THE SINGLE MOM'S
DEVOTIONAL

*Devotions to encourage the righteous practices
of a thriving single mom's home*

Belinda DeMuth, *General Editor*
Righteous Practice

From Righteous Practice

Righteous Practice is a DBA of bnbdemuth, LLC.

RighteousPractice.com provides blogs, videos, books that
will encourage all believers in Jesus Christ to take the
next best step in being more Christ like.

ISBN 978-1-09839-415-8 (Print)
ISBN 978-1-09839-416-5 (eBook)

I dedicate this devotional to the LORD, who pursued me for His good pleasure. Without the Father, introducing me to His Only Son, Jesus Christ I would have missed the blessings of mothering John, Isaac, and Anthony. May the Lord lead you men in the Godly calling of being husbands to Godly women and raising families that are a memorial to the power of salvation in Christ Jesus the Lord.

CONTENTS

INTRODUCTION

Growing up I only wanted to be a wife and mother. As I got closer to adulthood, I grew to like the idea of being a working wife and mother, but never a single mother. Raising my sons was an act of bravery most days that resulted in great successes as I learned to heal from failures. I intend to give you my notes on navigating your single parent household successfully being comfortable knowing your children will not lack good things.

When I came to salvation in Jesus Christ in 1998, I had a love for knowing Him in Spirit that led me to read Scripture, pray and apply the written Word the Bible to my parenting. As I looked to the LORD for direction in my parenting the focal points became pillars for me. The seven pillars are wisdom, understanding, security, purity, peace, provision, and support.

Webster's Dictionary reprinted in 1949 A **pillar** is defined as;

1) the supports of a building.
2) Things raised up as a memorial.

The memorial raised up is our Lord and Savior Jesus Christ on the cross at Calvary. Jesus is supporting us, the building or temple as Paul describes us in 1 Corinthians 6:19. The seven pillars were illuminated for me in Proverbs 9 that normally leads me to read Genesis chapter one often because God created the world with us in it in seven days. In Scripture the number seven represents completion. When I was raising sons, I had time usually in the morning for ten minutes with the LORD and that was it. This devotional is meant to be digested daily over seven weeks. Each day's devotional is meant to be read alongside your own Bible in ten minutes. At the end of each week ponder what you want your home to feel like, look like, even smell like. God is using this healing field of singleness for your good, mom. He brought you here for restoration, salvation, and success. What concerns you concerns God. As I craved more time with God, He found it and what great praise times I had with Him.

This devotional is focused on *you*, the single mom that is rarely recognized for needing practical guidance on how to lead a family in the Light of God. Church pastors and Bible study facilitators focus parenting sermons or group studies towards the normal family headed by a husband and a wife but, do not look to tailor these course studies that only have the mother as the leader of the home. This devotional is the sustenance you need to nourish your tired heart and mind so that you are energized for the valuable work you are doing in raising your family. The pillars of salvation I have listed below are:

Pillar One is Wisdom; 1 Corinthians 1:24 states that Christ the power of God is the wisdom of God. Successful single parenting requires agreement that you will ask the Lord Jesus Christ to be your Leader, causing your children to confidently follow you.

Pillar Two is Understanding; Proverbs 9:10 states, '*the fear of the LORD is the beginning of wisdom, and the knowledge of the Holy One is understanding*'.

Pillar Three is Security; Genesis 3:13 says, '*and the LORD God said to the woman, "What is this you have done?" the woman said, "The serpent deceived me, and I ate."* Boundaries must be put in place for your children and YOU. You the single parent are responsible to raise your children in safety in the fear of the LORD so that they will learn to trust themselves and care for others appropriately.

Pillar Four is Purity; Genesis 4:7 *"If you do well, will you not be accepted? And if you do not do well, sin lies at the door. And its desire is for you, but you should rule over it."* Single parenting used to be an unfortunate oddity brought on by death of the husband or the wife but, now it is too normal. Establish purity for your home by starting with yourself.

Pillar Five is Peace; John 14:27 *"Peace I leave with you, My peace I give to you; not as the world gives do I give to you. Let not your heart be troubled, neither let it be afraid."* If you are a believer of Christ Jesus the Son of God and Savior of the world then peace is your inheritance and worth passing on to your children.

Pillar Six is Provision; 1 Timothy 5:8 states, *'But if anyone does not provide for his own, and especially for those of his household, he has denied the faith and is worse than an unbeliever.'* God's word proclaims that money matters. I will give you the basics of budgeting, sacrificing and trusting for more using your hands and the LORD's favor.

Pillar Seven is Support; Ecclesiastes 4:12 says, *'Though one may be overpowered by another, two can withstand him. And a three-fold cord is not easily broken.'* Bring in others to partner with. Bring in loved ones that will bolster your desire and need for a stable home for you and your children. Married grandparents, aunts, uncles, co-workers and friends need to be around you and your children as their examples of selflessness will be vital to influence the same spirit within your own family unit.

WISDOM

1 Corinthians 1:23-24

*But we preach Christ crucified, to the Jews a
stumbling block and to the Greeks foolishness,
but to those who are called, both Jews and Greeks,
Christ is the power of God and the wisdom of God.*

Christ is the wisdom of God. You do not get to the point of life quicker that with verse 24, 'Christ is the power and wisdom of God'. Are you a believer in God the Father through His Only begotten Son, Jesus Christ? If not do pray,

"My God, I admit that I am a sinner. I believe that You gave Your one and only Son, Jesus Christ to die on the cross for my sins. I believe that You God raised Him from the dead and that He lives. I trust You Jesus, asking that you would forgive me of all my sins, come into my heart. Lead me in Your paths of righteousness."

Accepting Jesus Christ to be your Lord and Savior is the beginning of Wisdom and understanding Him is a daily revelation through the promptings of the Holy Spirit, your prayers and Bible reading. Praying this prayer for salvation is a done deal, mom; and life will continue to present you with challenges, but never again without victory on every side.

4

UNDERSTANDING

Proverbs 9:5-6

"Come, eat of my bread and drink of the wine
I have mixed. Forsake foolishness and live
and go in the way of understanding."

The way of understanding is Jesus Christ, God's one and only begotten Son. Christ is the wisdom of God and without the Savior, understanding our important station as single mothers will be missed. Put down that doughnut mom, pick up your Bible and read these two verses until your hunger is filled with His presence that satisfies you. Our children will learn that understanding God is equally balanced between agreement and acceptance. Our spirit agrees with God's Spirit that we are not almighty, so that we can accept that only with Holy Spirit will our might surface in us.

SECURITY

Proverbs 29:2

When the righteous are in authority, the people rejoice;
but when a wicked man rules, the people groan.

Moms, we owe it to our children to come to the saving grace of God's only Son, Jesus Christ; and become the righteousness of God.

Keeping our children safe does not mean we hover over them, removing all occasions for them to take leaps of faith that could fail. Keeping our children safe starts with not overusing the rod of correction. The American Academy for Pediatrics reports that 1 in 4 children are abused every year. Harming our children is despicable and deserving of legal correction.

Mom, if child abuse is in your history seek out a 12-step recovery group, Christian counselor, or even your child's pediatrician for help to end the cycle of abuse in your family. We owe it to our children to be a refuge from a messed-up world, NOT to contribute to their hardships!

PURITY

<u>1 Timothy 4:12</u>

*Let no one despise your youth, but be an example
to the believers in word, in conduct, in love,
in spirit, in faith, in purity.*

Do not allow another to despise you for your youth in this time of single parenting. Rejoice in being the example of God removing hindrances that did not glorify the pure and lovely children you get the privilege to lead in the way everlasting.

The definition of purity is sinlessness of life; and you, single mom are purity in motion. Your children will see your pure intentions for giving them life was indeed unselfish. They grow to value all life because all are made in the image of the Almighty God. Our precious babies are not mistakes; they are the outworking of obedience you possibly thought you lost. Keep your chin up, God loves you.

PEACE

Proverb 14:30

A sound heart is life to the body, but
envy is rottenness to the bones.

This is a great Proverb that focuses on the pillar of peace but also, the pillars support, security, understanding.

When I was a single mom, I spent a lot of time envying thinner women around me. This envy did not make me want to trim down my obese body, only overfeed it more and this exhausted the peace Christ died to give me.

Envy in other women robbed me of peace and friendships that I desired desperately at the time. The first avenue to peace the Holy Spirit put on my heart was to join the 12-Steps with Jesus Christ Bible Study at the church that has been my home for over a decade now. I had so many hurts in my past that kept me without peace and friendships but, going through that 12-step group made me look at the harm I was causing being envious of other women which in turn gave me a self-focus that caused me to overeat for protection.

I command you to find a 12-step group that can help you work through the hurts of your past. I suggest that you invite a woman that you have commonly been envious towards out for coffee and get to know her as an individual who might need you as a friend.

PROVISION

Genesis 22:8 w/ John 1:29

And Abraham said, "My son, God will provide
for Himself the lamb for a burnt offering."

• • •

The next day John saw Jesus coming toward him,
and said, "Behold! The Lamb of God who
takes away the sin of the world!"

Look at your current parenting style and ask yourself if you are making sacrifices that God has not asked you for? Now, look at your children and honestly ask yourself, 'what have my children sacrificed that God has not asked them for, but I imposed on them?'

Being fearful that God will not provide goes against His word as we see in these two verses. God will and has provided the Ultimate Sacrifice—Jesus Christ. Today, acknowledge honestly the job God did provide for you and the money you bring home from that job, and praise Him now for providing for you and your children. Thankfulness was missing in my career as a single parent when I began my venture and being unthankful caused me to make selfish money decisions that opened wholes of lack in my home. If you believe in Jesus Christ, you were forgiven all sin; the primary sin was not believing in God through His Only Son.

Before you can manage your money, first you must manage a lack of thankfulness for all God has provided you.

SUPPORT

Mark 14:29-30

Peter said to Him, "Even if all are made to stumble, yet I will not be." Jesus said to him, "Assuredly, I say to you that today, even this night before the rooster crows twice, you will deny Me three times."

Be alert mom, because being a woman of God is not without stumbles. In your relationship with Jesus Christ, you will fail to uphold Him, and yet He will recover you to Himself.

You lost your husband, boyfriend, and are broken from so much loss. Jesus knows how you feel because, He had the same heartbreak when His friend Peter did deny Him not just two times but, three times. Satan will use loneliness as a weapon to get us to deny our Savior.

Jesus Christ is our Redeemer and will lead us to thrive in our singleness with Him. He is the only Support that will give us life by forgiving us of our sins. Do not be afraid to be without a broken mate. Be fearful of missing the healing arms of your Almighty God.

Pillar to Ponder: Wisdom

Holy Spirit entered my space often before I would come to be saved by God's Son, Jesus Christ. We all know when a person enters a room, but we have not eyed them yet. Holy Spirit filled up space as any fleshed person you could see before you. In the mania I found myself in so often prior to salvation, He entered my room...me. God, the LORD cleaved to me when I would have outbursts of wrath against others or by myself. The call was the same, "Come." My answer to HIM, "No. Not now." I was so evil.

In August of 1998, I found myself with an unwanted pregnancy again. I worked for Kaufmann's Department Store and was quickly needing to know if I was pregnant again so that I could quickly make the appointment at the abortion clinic. You see, I had an abortion the prior August of 1997; I was in a rush to make sure nobody would ever know I exercised my "rights," and looked to repeat it. My live-in boyfriend did protest the first abortion, but I had rights and he was not going to control me. The abortion clinic refused to make an appointment for me this time, because the state passed a new law requiring a wait time once a clinic was notified of an intended abortion. Waiting would give time for others to see I was ill and wonder. Holy Spirit came into my restroom stall as I was in mania again, sobbing! I hated living with my boyfriend, and I hated that our son was always yelling at us to stop fighting. I did not have the mental capacity to have another baby with this man. Holy Spirit barked at me, "Leave the man! Keep this baby."

I went to my mother after work in mania and she loved me and helped me face, 'me', but with Him, Jesus Christ. Having my son was obedience to the LORD and He has rewarded me beyond all I could hope or think. I was a single mother and not forsaken or shamed. Whatever brought you to single parenting it was all to give God glory so that He could show off His unmerited favor on your life. The pillar of wisdom for this week will lead you to be saved by God the Father through His Only Son, Jesus Christ and you will receive Holy Spirit. Be born again dear heart. The prayer in the wisdom devotional this week will lead you to His highway of everlasting.

WISDOM

Proverbs 9:1

Wisdom has built her house, she has
hewn out her seven pillars;

When I came to the saving grace of Jesus Christ, I had an awakening. Or rather because of God awakening me to my corruptness, I could ask for the saving grace of His only Son, Jesus Christ. I had wisdom because, I took what I had knowledge of, God's Holy Spirit, and I acted on His promptings, and by faith I believed.

"Wisdom has built her house," means that she obtained a good foundation that her house could be rest on; and He was Jesus.

Seven represents completion in Scripture, coming from when God creating the world in seven days. Here, the woman having hewn out her seven pillars, are the things held in memorial that keep us leaning on the everlasting arms of the LORD.

These seven pillars were my focal points of salvation that God used to teach me how to run my home without an earthly husband, but with Him the Eternal Husband. The pillars are wisdom, understanding, security, purity, peace, provision, and support. The seven pillars stay upright on the firm foundation of God our Father and the Lord Jesus Christ, who left the Helper with us to guide us in all things. Selah

UNDERSTANDING

Ecclesiastes 7:12

For wisdom is a defense as money is a defense,
but the excellence of knowledge is that wisdom
gives life to those who have it.

Understanding is knowledge; that you comprehend exactly. When I was raising my sons, I resented that the parenting forums at churches was only meant for a two-parent household. The forums were meant to be performed by two people; a mother and a father of the children because the facilitator gave suggested parenting roles according to the established framework of the traditional home. In my resentment I took the parenting chores that were split up by the facilitator amongst the mother and father, and just did all of them. The LORD removed my resentment and gave me the resolution. Feeling sorry for my singleness was not allowed. I have knowledge but unless I put it to work, it would not be the wisdom I needed for a smooth-running home, let alone a fruitful life. If you get the opportunity to attend a parenting forum in your church, ask the facilitator to give you ways to make it work with a single parent in the home. We single moms must spearhead resolutions because, someone else probably could use the same help but, were too scared to ask.

SECURITY

Psalm 23:4

*Yea, though I walk through the valley of the shadow
of death, I will fear no evil; for You are with me;
Your rod and Your staff they comfort me.*

What is your 'valley of death?' Do you fear that your children will go hungry? Do you fear becoming homeless? Do you fear the lack of safety in your neighborhood or even failing? The LORD is with you in all these things, and as a woman saved by the blood of Christ, it is your legal obligation to ask God for mercy. Your Father does look out for you and keeps life from being too burdensome but, dear heart, do not forsake calling on Him for mercy.

There is a man named Job in the Bible that God called upright, and God allowed the devil to test him, to see if Job would curse Him. Job lost all his worldly possessions and every one of his ten children. Job even had an attack on his health. Job never once called out to God for mercy; and God was furious with Job over this.

Moms, we are His girls, His daughters; pray to God for mercy! Do you need more money coming into your home? Do you need a day without the kids under you? Do you need a hug? His justice requires God to fulfill your call for mercy. Security is having confidence in the One who saved us, to keep saving us time and again.

PURITY

1 Timothy 5:22

Do not lay hands on anyone hastily, nor share
in other people's sins; keep yourself pure.

I found lust exhausting when it lacked the fruit of godly marriage. Sexual desire outside the LORD's design of marriage is exhausting because, it is void of His blessing.

Ask yourself before you hastily lay hands on another, "is this worth my exhaustion?" "Is this worth possible rejection by this guy who is not my husband or even looking to be?"

Sexual sin is visible to Jesus Christ and while we are not condemned, Holy Spirit convicts us; "this is not good enough daughter." Keep yourself pure by removing the temptation of the person from your physical access. Pray and ask God for a friend's accountability to not waste your energy on lust.

Forsake sexual lust of any type. God's man is there for you, but make that man prove himself before you waste your energy. Keep yourself pure because He who is pure abides in you.

PEACE

Psalm 4:8

I will both lie down in peace, and sleep; for You alone,
O LORD, make me dwell in safety.

We single moms need peaceful sleep so that we are at our best for our families, employers, and God. Sleep has been proven to heal our bodies when injured or sick. Sleep inhibits fat storage which keeps us trim and energized. Sleep keeps us mentally sharp so that we can learn, pray, and teach others the will of God.

Look at your home, car, work area and see how these things keep you from having a good night's rest. When I had my last son, insomnia plagued me for over a decade. The year I filed for child support and divorce caused me to not sleep for a week, twice! My inability to sleep took a toll on my body because for once in my life, I could not keep weight on.

Talk to your doctor about a sleep protocol that will work best for you either with or without medication. I recommend treating your sleep preciously, just as you did for your children when they were babies. Set a time with your children for wrapping up their homework and getting dinner finished so there is plenty of time for you to settle into your bedtime routine. Take a soothing bath or shower, put on your favorite pajamas or robe, and make sure your feet are covered so they are warm and dry. Then read your Bible. Say your prayers, then put you and the kids to bed earlier than you are used to. Even if you only get to bed a half hour sooner, the routine will help you relax and to sleep more soundly for the time that you are in bed.

PROVISION

2 Thessalonians 3:10

For even when we were with you, we commanded you this: if anyone will not work, neither shall he eat.

Single mothers are the leaders of their families and as such, it is our responsibility to provide our children the sustenance they need to live. Being a single mother is not a license to perpetual poverty. We single mothers have ample family and friends that are more than willing to be of help, so that we can go to work and provide the money needed to make a good living for our children.

I challenge you to look at the job that you have and pray for the LORD to show you where extra money can be made with it. I know many single mothers tend to lean on health careers, and many hospitals will pay a shift differential, (that is a percentage increase on hourly pay) if you can work the emergency room or at off-peak times within your normal work week. If you work for a company that pays a monetary incentive or bonus for increased sales, do take the opportunity to obtain those sales. I have always worked in the financial industry and always opted for a sales position over a managerial position because the bonus incentives increased my take home pay far more than the higher manager's hourly rate. Do you have the opportunity for paid education with your company that could lead to advancement and higher pay? Go for it! Poverty is not a family heirloom, but a virus needing the vaccine of courage to kill it. Do not sell yourself short. God is with you and prosperity is a given as His children, not a surprise.

SUPPORT

<u>1 Peter 5:6</u>

Therefore humble yourselves under the mighty hand of God, that He may exalt you in due time, casting all your care upon Him, for He cares for you.

God cares for us. God cares for only you! Humbling yourself under the mighty hand of God, strengthens you for whatever the day brings.

Cast your cares on Him, for He cares for you; not like the world cares for you. The world wants everything in return for the lack luster pearls of help they throw at our feet. Do you find yourself bowing at the world's feet for crumbs that never satisfied you? The Lord is our Support of Excellence not poverty. Look to Him for strength to put forth a better day at work than you had yesterday. Look to Him for hugs that go clean through to your spirit, and not for hugs that only leave you hungrier.

Look to the Father to show you how to help your own son or daughter heal from the letdown of their own friends. We single moms are strong because our Support never fails.

Pillar to Ponder: Peace

It is time to enforce peace within your home. It may have been a traumatic breakup or divorce but surely you can see the opportunity in front of you to formulate peaceful tranquility. Start by finding a spot in your house or apartment that you can have quiet time with God. It may be the living room sofa, your bed, or an unused closet, but make it your space without exception. Get a blanket if needed or a heating pad if you lean on the cooler side of body temperature. Make sure your children know that when you are in your space, they must be quiet, knock only if it is an emergency, and then tell them how long you will be with God. Children want a calm and loving home and will make sure to help.

Look at your sleep both in quantity and quality. The peace devotional this week helps us depend on God for the peaceful sleep that rejuvenates us in safety. Setting a bedtime for the household will be undoable at first, but if you set the expectation with your children consistently, they will get on board and get to bed without a fuss. While the focus is on you the parent, do not be surprised when you experience your children being more compliant at home and in school with sweet sleep to spur them on.

A good sleep routine should have no electronics, comfortable clothing, a bedroom with the temperature best for your needs, and by all means, quiet. If quiet is not soothing; and for me as a kid quiet was not, use a white noise machine, a fan, or even a barely heard radio to help muffle any noise that may be outside your sleeping area. Quality sleep will keep anxiety down, overeating tamed, and keep you at the top of your game for a productive day of work.

Peace will mean letting go of things that block you from it. Such as people, social media, your car and the hurts of your past.

WISDOM

Luke 7:35

"But wisdom is justified by her children."

Jesus was speaking to the Pharisees, that their wisdom is shown in their works or in this case their wording, "children". The same outworking of my wisdom was justified in the effectiveness of my parenting.

Children growing up with a single mother are not destined to have broken families that are slaves to poverty, on the contrary. Children of single mothers should be even more, hardworking and grateful citizens with testimonies of their great and awesome LORD, making highways of holiness through the deserts of a fallen world.

Children of a single mother should have days' worth of testimonies of God saving them from toxic foes and replenishing them with life giving devotees. Our children should look forward to marrying strong and tenderhearted wives or husbands, who will help shepherd in a world of children who boast in God the Father, who satisfies their souls.

UNDERSTANDING

Job 32:8

But there is a spirit in man, and the breath of the Almighty gives him understanding.

An aspect of understanding is an intelligence between two or more persons. No, not you and God; but God the Father, God the Son, God the Holy Spirit, **and** you. You have One God, who is three persons meant to be worshipped by us single moms in the operation of our homes, our families, and ourselves.

Single parenting is not broken parenting. I finally gave up worshipping a broken man and turned to worshipping the Man, my LORD.

I gave up letting my sons see their mother chunking up on cookies over a man who was perfectly happy without us. I gave up allowing my children to go hungry waiting on a father to bring home groceries, when he could not bring himself home. I got understanding and then my children got their lucid, happy, and thinned out mother back. I got Life and there is no turning back.

SECURITY

Psalm 18:2

The LORD is my rock and my fortress and my deliverer;
My God, my strength, in whom I will trust;
My shield and the horn of my salvation, my stronghold.

The LORD is my protector, deliverer, and stronghold, so whom do, I fear? Without God in Christ, any security measures put in place to protect our family and home is futile.

Webster's Dictionary describes security as the freedom from danger or risk. Do you think becoming a single mother was anything but, the freedom from danger or risk? Take heart mom, God is with you in the healing field called single parenting. Broken marriages and relationships are a two-way street and yet, God saw it to be our salvation. For some of us single parenting lasts a short while and for others it is always, but so long as we are going with the LORD we are delivered to safety.

1 Corinthians 6:9-11

*Do you not know that the unrighteous will not
inherit the kingdom of God? Do not be deceived.
Neither fornicators, nor idolaters, nor adulterers,
nor homosexuals, nor sodomites, nor thieves,
nor covetous, nor drunkards, nor revilers, nor extortioners
will inherit the kingdom of God, and such were some
of you. But you were washed, but you were sanctified,
but you were justified in the name of the Lord Jesus
and by the Spirit of our God.*

Take heart mom, if you have accepted Jesus Christ as Savior and Lord of your life, then you are washed, sanctified, and justified. You have a new lineage thanks to our Lord Jesus, becoming the perfect and only acceptable sacrifice, to make you righteous in God's eyes. Perfect is not your focus, Christ Jesus must be! For when we put our eyes on His perfect sacrifice that not a one could ever out do, then we are virgin again, honest again, sober again, and pure. See the purity you are, ONLY because Jesus Christ paid the sin debt in full on a tree on Calvary. Pass this word onto your children today, so they know the power of purity Jesus Christ has given them in being saved by His precious blood.

PEACE

John 14:27

*"Peace I leave with you, My peace I give to you;
not as the world gives do I give to you. Let not your heart
be troubled, neither let it be afraid."*

Our households are to be places of peace for our families and so often chaos can rule our private places. As the head of household, we moms are responsible to enforce peace for our children and ourselves, so that the whole family is able to rest. Look at your home and find ways to encourage peacefulness with the furnishings, entertainment sources, and the company everyone keeps. Jesus Christ gave you His peace and fear must be put on the run. Selah!

PROVISION

Genesis 22:12-14

And He said, "Do not lay your hand on the lad, or do anything to him; for now, I know that you fear God, since you have not withheld your son, your only son, from Me." Then Abraham lifted his eyes and looked, and there behind him was a ram caught in the thicket by its horns. So, Abraham went and took the ram, and offered it up for a burnt offering instead of his son. And Abraham called the name of the place, The-LORD-Will-Provide; as it is said to this day, "In the Mount of the LORD it shall be provided.

Mom, your sacrifice to give birth to your child apart from marriage is being rewarded by the LORD, because He knows that you did not forsake His child's life to save your own. I did abort one of my children and it was the worst year for me, my three-year-old son, and his father. But God did give me a do-over exactly one year later and I was not going to repeat that mistake. I did have that baby, my Isaac and because of him, I did ask the Father's Son, Jesus Christ to save me from my sins and forgive me. The LORD has not ceased to provide abundantly for me, my sons, and any that I get the privilege to be in the company of. Provision is all encompassing and as a single mom look up to your Provider and thank Him that you are strong and chose life over death because you saw that greater LIFE would be had.

SUPPORT

Exodus 33:14-15

And He said, "My Presence will go with you, and I will give you rest." Then he said to Him, "If Your Presence does not go with us, do not bring us up from here."

Divorcing my first husband was a decision that took years for me to do because, I could not see in God's Word justification to do so. God Almighty, gave me many signs that He **had** found wrong with this husband and that He the LORD, was done with the marriage my husband abandoned. The final year of marriage was the most treacherous for me, my sons, and now my parents because I withdrew an order for child support payments hoping for reconciliation with my estranged husband. That final year was almost the death of me, as I had contemplated driving my car into a tree on a desperate drive home from work. I had no money to buy groceries to feed my sons, or me, or my parents; but I did have life insurance. We were given groceries from a local church that night and for many nights and days after. I buckled down in making a grocery budget that stretched my pays. More importantly, I refiled for child support payments and after six months was provided money with garnished payments from my soon to be ex-husband. Legal support is God's provision for you and your children!

Pillar to Ponder: Security

Single mothers are the leaders of their homes and securing it makes your house or apartment a home. You and your children must feel safe so that you can love and praise the Lord God Almighty without wavering; in this healing from divorce and abandonment will be had.

Single mothers must not allow men they are not married to, to spend the night in their homes. I raised three boys as a single parent, and never did I allow a man I wasn't married to, to spend the night or to be in my home once the sun went down. Men will take advantage of a mother in harmful ways and as a Christian we must not allow room for another to sin against us.

If you are raising sons, you must encourage them to be leaders and that way they will grow up wanting to lead businesses and homes with loving wives and children in a fashion that honors God. If you are raising daughters, you must be the example of putting first things first, marriage before any sexual relationship. When we came to faith in the Father through His Son Jesus Christ, His purity purified us.

Securing the home means setting boundaries for you the parent and this makes the children feel safe in trusting you and obeying you. This boundary of no sexual activity within your home keeps the children safe from male predators; again, God holds you the single mother responsible to keep you and the children safe from harm. The US Constitution's Second Amendment affords law abiding citizens to maintain a gun in the home for protection. Do look to your state for the laws to be applied if you choose to use a firearm in the home. A security system is another way to secure your home from predators and you want to make sure all your children are trained in how to use all devices of home security for when you are away. Assess the proper locks are on the doors and windows of your home. Post the phone numbers to the safety departments in your immediate vicinity onto your refrigerator, for all to see clearly. Take charge mom and your children will follow your Godly example. Securing your home, children, and person is the model of this week's security devotional to remind us God is our deliverer and protector.

WISDOM

Proverbs 24:3-4

Through wisdom a house is built, and by understanding it is established: by knowledge the rooms are filled with all precious and pleasant riches.

Wisdom must have action in order to be useful. Faith in our heavenly Father is the action that matters and will fill the spaces of your heart with precious gladness. Mom, you are not alone. In the cool of the evening, we see that there is not a husband to snuggle up to. Put aside the temptation to feel sorry for yourself. I ask you to take that feeling of being alone and get your kids together for a family game night or family movie night and get all laughing. Fill your lonely heart with the bountiful blessing of your happy family all around you while filling the kids' minds with memories worth keeping.

Being a single mother may be new for you and wisdom will be the cornerstone that your home must be set on. See the harvest of understanding that your Father God has set up for you in the healing field of singleness you are set in.

UNDERSTANDING

<u>1 Corinthians 12:17-20</u>

If the whole body were an eye, where would be the hearing? If the whole were hearing, where would be the smelling? But now God has set the members, each one of them, in the body just as He pleased. And if they were all one member, where would the body be? But now indeed there are many members, yet one body.

Being the head of a single parent home is by no means the environment to sow pity. God needs every member in order for the body of Christ, (the church) to work properly therefore, rejoice. God gave us this singleness because at this time in our lives and our children's lives any other persons would only hinder us from His blessings. We single moms are needed examples of outrageous praise reports pointing to this Almighty and Amazing LORD! Pity parties are not the foundation for our homes and God needs us and our children to show the way of victory in adversity to the other members of the body of Christ.

SECURITY

Genesis 3:13

And the LORD God said to the woman,
"What is this you have done?" The woman said,
"The serpent deceived me, and I ate."

God set up a clear boundary for Adam and Eve in the garden but, instructed Adam, *"...the tree of the knowledge of good and evil you shall not eat."* God set this boundary because to not obey Him would cause Adam and Eve to die. What boundary is needed in your home that you, mom, are not setting up? The security system of a single mom's home relies on boundaries that promote safety for our children and us. Guarding our minds from the deception of sin is found in prayer and reading our Bibles. We think about our children needing curfews but, what about us? Curfews limit the time our children spend with friends so as, to hopefully limit times of getting into trouble. That curfew works for us too. Putting a curfew on our own time with friends makes our children trust us to make good decisions and helps them feel safe knowing mom is never too far out of reach if they need help.

PURITY

Genesis 4:7

*"If you do well, will you not be accepted?
And if you do not do well, sin lies at the door. And its
desire is for you, but you should rule over it."*

Purity for us single parents begins with repentance of sin and acknowledging that salvation in Jesus Christ, purifies us from the stains sin left on and in us. Coming into single parenthood **is not** sinful in and of itself but is God's healing field for our past hurts from relationships that did not glorify Him, thereby not good enough for us. Pure is beautiful. Pure is sacrificial. Pure is us redeemed.

PEACE

Matthew 5:9

*"Blessed are the peacemakers, for they
shall be called sons of God."*

Webster's Dictionary says that a peacemaker is one who makes peace by reconciling parties that are at variance or at odds with one another. At the heart of the word peace is freedom. Freedom from war; hostility; public quiet. Freedom from mental agitation, public tranquility. The reason I became a single parent was because my husband was an agitator of my mind, fueled hostility via abandonment and adultery, and my worry was very apparent! To be a peacemaker meant that I had to face the fact that my husband did not have the skills to be my husband or a father; and I had to live life without him. I had to quiet my sons, especially my oldest; by encouraging him to let his father go and find a good life without him. Watching my son sort out his broken heart is what God used to quiet me. Holy Spirit would speak, "hush, John will live through this heartache, if I stop eating the cookies and make myself available to him, if he wants to talk to me." Peace means that we can give God the harms done to us realizing that it is okay to let the broken be broken, if that is allowed by my Father. Your heavenly Father loves those babies of yours more than you could ever hope or think. Now, put down those cookies! Get at the edge of your bed and pray for your child's broken heart to be healed and sealed by the Holy Spirit.

PROVISION

Genesis 41:34-36

"Let Pharaoh do this, and let him appoint officers over the land to collect one-fifth of the produce of the land of Egypt in the seven plentiful years. And let them gather all the food of those good years that are coming, and store up grain under the authority of Pharaoh, and let them keep food in the cities. Then that food shall be as a reserve for the land for the seven years of famine which shall be in the land of Egypt, that the land may not perish during the famine."

Mom, prioritize keeping $1000 in your savings account, at all times. If $1000 is overwhelming then make $5oo the got-to amount in your savings account, at all times.

I moved my sons, parents, and I from the inner city of Cleveland out to the cornfields of Montville and for the first five years I had three occasions when my $1000 got eaten. Those three occasions were Super Storm Sandy taking off my roof; the family car that my new driver smashed backing out of our garage; and the spring melt that flooded my basement. My oldest son would complain all the time when I cracked down on saving saying, "we never get to do anything with your bonuses mom, just save for a rainy day!" And I would always say with a whip of sarcasm, "because it always rains on our house." Mom, you are going to have a future and if you make saving for a rainy day a habit, you will squash the fear of 'what if?" Being a single mother should not mean poverty! God Almighty is your better half and lack is not what He is about.

SUPPORT

James 5:16

Confess your trespasses to one another, and pray for one another, that you may be healed. The effective, fervent prayer of a righteous man avails much.

James teaches in this verse the power of praying for another as a healing for ourselves. Wow! Mom, if you are a believer in the Lord Jesus Christ and accepted Him filling you with the Holy Spirit, then you are a righteous woman and your prayers avail much.

The pillar of salvation, support, is about obtaining it so that you can give it. Building healthy relationships requires that we obtain the skill of giving and receiving but often the breakdown of relationships comes from a lopsided behavior of always giving or always taking.

Get involved with a small group Bible study at your church so that you can learn about being supportive but on a small scale. If childcare makes going to a small group Bible study challenging, then offer to hold the study in your home; being the place for others to acquire the skill of being supportive. At the same time opening your home improves your own skills on being a source of support and friendship for those in need.

Pillar to Ponder: Purity

When we became born again through the saving grace of Jesus Christ, we were made pure. Being Christ like is the outworking of this purity and renewing the mind in prayer and reading your Bible will renew your heart and this increases your beauty. Being a single mother is a hardship when it first happens, and healing requires space. I do not recommend having a romantic relationship with a man for the first six months because you need space and time to dream about the home you would like to have that you are leading. Establish the needed communication between you, your children, and their extended family members to mend any fences that fell during your breakup. Purity needs strength and sexual lust robs you of strength mentally, physically, and spiritually. Think about the kind of woman you want to be in your singleness and achieve your goals; but you cannot see when you are all about someone else's needs. When you are ready to date set a curfew for yourself to keep a man's contact with you restrained. When you are getting to know a man sex will bring out all sorts of idiotic behavior that men carry around, but when you make the man wait the idiotic behavior shows up much sooner. Without sex you or even your children will not have an emotional attachment and can leave idiot to himself much more easily. While you are a single mother read your Bible because when a father is not in the home your oldest son, not daughter, needs to be given some burden of leadership and protector. Purity is a shield of protection you will be happy God gave you.

WISDOM

Proverbs 1:20-21

Wisdom calls aloud outside, she raises her voice
in the open squares. She cries out in the chief concourses,
at the openings of the gates in the city she speaks
her words; "How long, you simple ones will you love
simplicity? For scorners delight in their scorning,
and fools hate knowledge."

King Solomon is known to be the writer of the Proverbs, and the highest quality of a human who was created by God is wisdom, of which is given a feminine prudence.

King Solomon saw in his own father, King David's example that insecurity within a family and a kingdom ruins all wise actions. Fools purposefully corrupt all good things in life, albeit morality, homes, money, and even children. We single moms must refrain from the temptation of being foolish in the leading of our households and trying to be self-sufficient in our own power. Cling to Almighty God in good days and especially challenging ones, so as not to lose sensitivity to the Holy Spirit's promptings. His promptings is your wisdom to help you steer your household in knowledge and safety.

UNDERSTANDING

Proverbs 3:5-6

Trust the LORD with all your heart, and lean not on your own understanding; in all your ways acknowledge Him, and He will direct your paths."

Remember, that understanding is an agreement of the mind between two or more persons. Single parenting is not without the LORD to put you on a straight and smooth path. This proverb that says to 'acknowledge Him,' means to remember Him. I want you to pray before you make decisions about parenting, work, or dating; but God will still be your sounding board if you need help after you made a decision. Is the decision not going as planned, call out to God to help you, and He will.

Acknowledging God is understanding that His way is best because He created us. He created you to understand that you do not have all the answers. God has provided you help from parents, pastors, siblings, friends, bosses, and more importantly, the Holy Spirit. The Holy Spirit abides in you, and every place you go, the ground on which you stand is holy. Your children will thrive when you put your trust in Him, because they will trust Him too. Remember Him to direct your paths.

SECURITY

Genesis 28:15

"Behold, I am with you and will keep you wherever you go, and will bring you back to this land; for I will not leave you until I have done what I have spoken to you."

'Keep' in this verse is similar in meaning to a guard, some-one that protects another. The LORD protects the home of a single mother just at He does a married mother. Please dismiss any inse-curity you might have in God protecting you.

The security of your home begins with securing your mind from the thoughts that God is punishing you and your children for any mistakes you made. Salvation is freedom from the care of sins, the Lord Jesus Christ saved you from.

Security means to guard your heart from harmful relation-ships, and to have hope that marriage will work for you as God intends, if you are courageous to venture there again.

Security is confident in the freedom of carelessness from the concerns of this world. What is your greatest need today? Sit on your bed and talk or pray to your Father for what you need, and He will fill it. As today's verse promises, 'I am with you and will keep you wherever you go.'

PURITY

Romans 12:2

And do not be conformed to this world, but be transformed by the renewing of your mind, that you may prove what is that good and acceptable and perfect will of God.

Purity is the freedom from guilt and the defilement of sin, it is innocence. Purity is removed of any excess, as the excess is never sustainable without help. That is what our relationship with God tutors us in; laying aside the excess of the world for the sustainable Word of God that saves us.

The world in its perfection is uninteresting and only the Bible, God's inspired Word will renew your mind so that you can comprehend His perfect will. Purity of heart makes us agree with His Spirit and we are transformed into the likeness of Christ from glory to glory. This is the transformation He purposed, that would only be had for us on the highway of single parenting.

PEACE

Matthew 10:34

"Do not think that I came to bring peace on earth.
I did not come to bring peace but a sword,"

The word peace is used in legal terms such as, 'Hold your peace,' 'Keep the peace,' and most often Scripture uses, 'Peace of God.'

The law affords our rights to peace whether it is in our homes, businesses, and even our person. Peace is owed to our person legally so that we have spiritual calm. As a single parent the law is your partner of sorts, to force outsiders to leave you in peace.

The petition for child support is meant to force your ex-husband to provide for his children so that you have peace to raise them apart from worry over their provisions. The separation agreement is a legal document that forces that ex-husband to leave your home because his presence does not foster peace in the house, the finances, or relationships with you and his children. The visitation agreement is the document that sets the rules of how your ex-husband is to keep a peaceful relationship with his children. And the restraining order is your commitment to no longer allow your ex-husband to physically harm you or your children.

Your Bible is the legal document between you and Jesus Christ the Lord, that He will never leave you or forsake you, as He is your peace, now and forever more.

PROVISION

1 Timothy 5:8

*But if anyone does not provide for his own,
and especially for those of his household, he has denied
the faith and is worse than an unbeliever.*

I removed a child support order because my husband and children's father promised to come home and provide for us.

My husband lied, he never came home, and he did not provide for us. I got in the way of God disciplining my husband by removing the child support order and in turn I and my sons got the discipline.

It is wrong to save anyone from God's discipline, as if we are kinder gods. I promptly refiled the child support order but this time it took longer and many days we had to get food from the church food pantry in our township. Nine months after the second and last filing I walked out of court grateful to God for the award of child support so that I could now feed my sons.

My stern recommendation is that any child support order started or now in place, never remove it. The sheer need to get the courts to intervene and make your husband do the minimum of providing for his family, is for the salvation of his soul. Do not get in the way of God disciplining your husband, lest the discipline come to you and your children.

SUPPORT

Ruth 1:15-16

And she said, "Look, your sister-in-law has gone back to her people and to her gods; return after your sister-in-law." But Ruth said; "Entreat me not to leave you, or to turn back from following after you; for wherever you go, I will go; and wherever you lodge, I will lodge; your people shall be my people, and your God, my God."

When I was a single mother, I longed for God to find me a good husband. Instead, God gave me new friendships with married women who were married to men of God that I could study. Ruth has the dedication for her mother-in-law and now friend, Naomi that I am blessed to have in my friends Kathy and Marlene.

My Father God got forehead to forehead with me when I was getting ready for a first date with the man who would become my husband and He said, "he will never be Me." I took my Lord's revelation to heart and gained perspective of human limitations when it came to relationships. I studied my friends' marriages and they had good days and bad days but more importantly they had God. I did enjoy dating my husband and thoroughly delighted in being married to this man of God. And yet my Ben, would never be God. Ben loved God so much that many days I was jealous of the attention God was getting from Ben that I wanted! God is my Abba. God is my Friend indeed. And a husband will never be God so, lean into Him. Your Support is The LORD in Christ and filled with His Holy Spirit, you will never again walk alone.

Pillar to Ponder: Understanding

Think of understanding as a fruit of the Spirit. As you spend time with the Father in prayer and reading your Bible understanding and knowledge are ever increased. We that are born again and filled with the Holy Spirit are prompted by Him to pray and read our Bibles thereby maturing our spirituality. You and God, because you are saved have an agreement of mind that makes His will understood by you. At times I feel and voice to the Lord, "reading Psalm 23, again." Each reading of your Bible births new revelation and often it may not be written in your Bible. Make no mistake however, that what is written in your Bible is what God intends for you to implement in order to have blessing from Him. Cohabitation is very common with single mothers, but honestly it is twisted to live with a man you are not married to. God gave you, the single mother, the charge of your household and only when God allows you to marry again are you then allowed to divert leadership duties to your new husband. Your Bible tells you how to raise a man who will be a strong and loving husband and then father. The Holy Spirit will reveal certainty of an action to take when certainty is lacking either because you need more maturity or need more time to heal.

WISDOM

Proverbs 10:14

*Wise people store up knowledge, but the mouth
of the foolish is near destruction.*

A fool is described as a person who purposefully corrupts good counsel or good behaviors. The mouth of the foolish being near destruction, is resounded by James 1:26 that warns to bridle the tongue for it will corrupt the speaker and its hearers. As a single mother you can trust that God is on your side and will lead you to implement disciplines for your children that will encourage them to dream for the impossible while working on making the impossible realized.

The Holy Spirit will prompt you on what to pray while giving you guidance on how to pray. The Holy Spirit will reveal to you, the attributes of Him that you value most, so that you continue to seek Him consistently with power, knowing that He will fulfill your desires.

PROVISION

Acts 20:33-34

"I have coveted no one's silver or gold or apparel. Yes, you yourselves know that these hands have provided for my necessities, and for those who were with me."

When I was married to my first husband, I could not understand why he took no delight in providing for our sons. I rejoiced in giving my sons brand new clothes, especially at Easter time. My sons were so excited to go with me to the Children's Place and find the nicest pants sets that would light up their charming faces and then later the same outfit would be a way of cleaning up for a barbecue down the line into summer. I know the pride the Apostle Paul felt in having more than enough work, so as not to covet another's silver, gold, or Easter outfits. Another occasion to display my provision to my children, was to make my oldest son, who was not more than ten years old at the time, accompany me to the symphony for a Christmas concert. My oldest son and I got dressed in our Sunday best for this Saturday night concert. We dined before the concert at the symphony hall's restaurant that did not allow for the serving of soda pop to my son and instead, he ordered a cappuccino. My son to this day talks about our date and the astonishment of a restaurant not allowing the serving of soda pop. Do not take for granted the opportunity of showing your children the blessing that providing for them is. In this you will inspire them to be delighted at the chance to display their provision for their own families one day, knowing that God's favor is towards them all the days of their lives.

SUPPORT

<u>Exodus 17:11-12</u>

And so it was, when Moses held up his hand, that Israel prevailed; and when he let down his hand, Amalek prevailed. But Moses' hands became heavy; so they took a stone and put it under him, and he sat on it. And Aaron and Hur supported his hands, one on one side, and the other on the other side; and his hands were steady until the going down of the sun.

As a single mother you will need support from others, so you become confident in this great undertaking. Do not be over-whelmed at all the balls you are juggling; obtain friendships that will help you to keep the balls in the air and prevail against the evil one. I encourage you to become part of a church near your home because an important skill that a single mother needs is to show up for others in need.

When I became a single parent, I had many needs and others did help me but, the Holy Spirit put it on me to look at others in need and help them. When I attended Alcoholics Anonymous and Overeaters Anonymous, the twelve steps taught that once my need for healing was met, keeping that healing would be dependent on helping another to obtain healing for themselves. That is show up for others. Moses had power in his hands to subdue the war brought by Amalek, but he could not do it alone. Aaron and Hur had to help keep Moses' hands steadily raised up; to come along side Moses and all prevailed against Amalek. As a single mother you are needing to prevail against the stain of poverty because it cripples the finances, of course, but moreover poverty cripples our spirits.

Pillar to Ponder: Provision

It is time to give the LORD Almighty praise for providing for you and your children! Thank God for your healthy body. Most single mothers have more good health than money however, without a healthy body you cannot show up to your job to make the money you need. Yes, praise Him now. God promises to provide for us and yet we may find that we still do not have enough money after a family breaks up. See how your current job can help you make more money. Perhaps if you are a shift worker ask your boss about a different shift that possibly pays more. If you are a nurse look to your employing hospital for departments that pay more for the same nursing duties, like the emergency room. Are you in the financial industry, then you have many opportunities to increase your take home pay with sales bonuses? Will you need to get a promotion to a supervisory position to increase your pay? Start applying for all open positions within your company even if you are not yet qualified. I have not worked for a company that did not provide feedback with training if I applied for a promotion but, I did not fit the billet at the time. Be encouraged when training is offered to you by your managers and thank them for helping you be ready for the next time that better position is available. It is also time to look at your household expenses on paper. Write down the monthly payments for anything that appears on your credit bureau. Credit bureau payments are required obligations.

The priorities of the budget to coincide with the credit obligations are home, (rent or mortgage payment), car note, student loan, credit cards, and medical bills. As a single mother make it a goal to get these credit bureau obligations to equal 50% or less of your take home pay. Train the utilities to equal 20% or less of take-home pay; 10% or that pay needs to be for living life; 10% needs to be saved. See my website righteouspractice.com in the Single Mom Hangout for tips on keeping your home monetarily happy.

WISDOM

Proverbs 9:10

"The fear of the LORD is the beginning of wisdom, and the knowledge of the Holy One is understanding."

Fear of the LORD is the beginning of wisdom because Christ is God's wisdom, (1 Corinthians 1:24). Fear in this verse is not a regret of the encounter but, a respect for the encounter.

A single mother is successful in the running of her home when she recognizes that the LORD is her better half. Your Bible is what parenting books try to base their counsel on but, still miss the mark because those books look to raise the pride of the doctor's expertise of which is foolishness in God's eyes.

Knowledge of the Holy One is understanding that we moms are smart enough to discern right from wrong and good from evil. Wisdom is not useful until it is worked out by the decisions a mother makes to keep her family and home happy, healthy, and safe.

UNDERSTANDING

2 Timothy 2:7

Consider what I say, and may the Lord give you understanding in all things.

One of the meanings I found in my Webster's Dictionary regarding understanding is, 'union of sentiments; as a good understanding between a minister and His people.'

The Holy Spirit is our union of sentiments. The only sentiment that matters is that we believe Jesus Christ went to the cross for us once, and He is not doing it again.

We will accept His perfect sacrifice as the finished work it is, or we will not. The break-up of a family through divorce was a joint effort, as is, being forgiven by our Father through His Son.

Just as we single moms had to let that marriage go for various reasons we too had to choose to be bound with the Savior or not. Our understanding that what the devil intended for evil, God used to preserve our lives is the perfection of sentiments between us and our Minister.

SECURITY

Deuteronomy 17:19-20

*And it shall be with him, and he shall read it
all the days of his life, that he may learn to fear the
LORD his God and be careful to observe all the words
of this law and these statutes, that his heart may not
be lifted above his brethren, that he may not turn aside
from the commandment to the right hand or to the left,
and that he may prolong his days in his kingdom,
he and his children in the midst of Israel.*

Our children rely on our leadership to be steady so, as to fearlessly follow us. We moms are to read God's word the Bible and do what it says to do. Security begins with you the parent being trustworthy. This Scripture from the Old Testament gives accounts of a king's reign only being as successful as the security he provides his subjects. Just like a people can only follow a king that puts their safety first, so it is for our children in following us.

PURITY

Mark 2:21-22

"No one sews a piece of unshrunk cloth on an old garment; or else the new piece pulls away from the old, and the tear is made worse. And no one puts new wine into old wineskins; or else the new wine bursts the wine-skins, the wine is spilled, and the wineskins are ruined. But new wine must be put into new wineskins."

Learning sexual purity as a single mom is your right and duty as God's daughter in Christ. Purity in sex is easy when the surroundings demand nothing but adherence however, American society demands the abandonment of all sexual purity as though you have no right to expect such luxury. Sexual purity is a luxury I demanded and yet failed at sometimes, until my husband Ben saved me from the effort in marriage.

Sexual purity is had when our heart is changed by salvation through Jesus Christ our righteousness; so that our mind is free to desire purity's luxury. Single mom please set boundaries for yourself so that the luxury of purity is realized.

These were rules for me that I lend to you. Forbid any men to sleep with you in your home. Never stay overnight in a man's home. Never make your children wonder when you will be home from a date. Set up with your children the person you will be out with, where the two of you will go, and the time they will expect to see you home in your own bed sleeping. Men need to know that being with these kids' mom for any reason is a luxury.

PEACE

<u>Romans 5:1-2</u>

Therefore, having been justified by faith, we have peace with God through our Lord Jesus Christ, through whom also we have access by faith into this grace in which we stand, and rejoice in hope of the glory of God.

Being a single mother does not make us a stain on society. We that believe in the Lord Jesus Christ are justified by our faith in Him and have peace with the Father.

Do you know and accept mom, that you have no enemy in God? By faith we have access into this grace in which we stand. This grace by which we stand is our unmerited favor an irrevocable gift. We did not work for this grace and to think we should try is to display the iniquity of pride.

Now dear heart take charge of your home and family and think about what kind of leader you want to be. What kind of woman have you always wanted to aspire to? In Christ you are well and can stand tall knowing that you are approved by God because of Christ the Lord abiding with you.

PROVISION

Exodus 15:26

*"If you diligently heed the voice of the LORD your God,
and do what is right in His sight, give ear to His
commandments and keep all His statutes, I will put none
of the diseases on you which I have brought on
the Egyptians. For I am the LORD who heals you."*

One of the names of God is Jehovah Rapha, which means the "LORD who heals you." Single moms sometimes are known for meager funds but not meager good health. Thank God for strong backs to sit up straight and make those sales calls. Thank God for strong legs to stand at the register and ring out that line of customers, or for strong arms to put those library books back in place on the shelves, or for the increased mental focus that allowed you to ace that college exam that will get you the promotion at the bank. God is good!

SUPPORT

Ecclesiastes 4:11-12

Again, if two lie down together, they will keep warm;
but how can one be warm alone? Though one may be
overpowered by another, two can withstand him.
And a threefold cord is not quickly broken.

As a single mom I was grateful for all the family I had to help me in raising my sons. I set the rules and my parents or sisters consistently helped me be accountable to live with the outcomes. For a short while my middle sister lived with me and my sons and one time my oldest son was out past curfew, and I had to discipline him. My sister was the support I needed to not let the matter go but, to follow through with the appropriate punishment. Sometimes grounding our children is as hard on us moms as it is on the kids but, God expects us to be the leader He purposed us to be for our children. Thank the LORD for giving us family to lean on.

Pillar to Ponder: Support

I have been a banker since the day I had to accept being a single parent. In my career I prosper when I ask my partners, i.e., financial advisors, mortgage officers, private banker, and commercial bankers to assist me in meeting my customer's needs. These partners are my support system. If you are new to single parenting or if you are looking to not have so much struggle with the single life you've been in, then get support. Start with being part of a church. I do not recommend dating more than a couple of churches a month. I attend two churches because my youngest son chose his own church when he became an adult and moved out of my home, so visiting him happens at his church. Both churches are in rural communities, and they are night and day as far as who attends but both teach and apply Scripture as it is written. This is vital! Many churches have small groups or what you may know as a Bible Study group, and these groups are for all to get to know others and be of support for each other in the faith. Small groups are where you learn to care about another and receive care. Small groups can focus on parenting, marriage, divorce recovery, financial independence, alcoholism and drug addiction, home schooling, books of the Bible, business networking, etc. I recommend attending a twelve-step program to help you get your hurt in order with God's leadership. What I mean is that we moms, will think we are in all this pain and not consider what this always broken, or newly broken family has done to our children. A twelve-step program will put co-dependency to rest quickly so that we focus on helping our children heal allowing them to be productive for God's glory.

ABOUT THE AUTHOR

Belinda DeMuth is the owner of Righteous Practice an online website where she writes blogs and makes videos about the application of Scripture to life, so you the Christian obtain confidence that you are getting your walk with the Lord Jesus Christ right. At the website Righteous Practice you will find the Single Mom Hangout where Belinda produces videos to lend single mothers her notes on running a successful single parent home.

Belinda has three sons, (two naturally and one gifted to her). All her sons are grown with good jobs, fine reputations in their township, and looking to find special women to make their own brides someday. On August 13, 2016, Belinda married Benjamin DeMuth and made a home in Chardon, Ohio. In sorrow and joy Belinda had to give her husband Benjamin back to God on June 29, 2020, becoming a widow. Belinda enjoys running, traveling, reading, and making memories with her extended family.